W9-CNX-504

EXTREME CAREERS™

MANGA ARTISTS

Tamra Orr

rosen publishing's
rosen central®

New York

Published in 2009 by The Rosen Publishing Group, Inc.
29 East 21st Street, New York, NY 10010

Copyright © 2009 by The Rosen Publishing Group, Inc.

First Edition

Library of Congress Cataloging-in-Publication Data

Orr, Tamra.
Manga artists / Tamra Orr.
    p. cm.—(Extreme careers)
Includes bibliographical references and index.
ISBN-13: 978-1-4042-1854-3 (library binding)
1. Comic books, strips, etc.—Japan—Juvenile literature. 2. Cartooning—Japan—Juvenile literature. 3. Comic books, strips, etc.—Vocational guidance—United States—Juvenile literature. 4. Cartooning—Vocational guidance—United States—Juvenile literature. I. Title.
NC1764.5.J3O77 2008
741.5'952—dc22
                                                      2007050666

Manufactured in Malaysia

Contents

Introduction

Hey, you! Yes, you . . . the one standing to the side in the manga aisle reading your fifth book in a row. We see you. We've been watching. You've been there for almost a half hour now. If no one bothers you, we bet you'll be there for at least another thirty minutes. Of course, you aren't alone. The entire aisle is lined with more people just like you. Each one of you is practicing *tachiyomi*—the Japanese term for "stand reading." The people in Japan do it, too, which is why they have a specific name for it. The Japanese stand in the aisle to read their favorite manga series just like you do. In fact, they do it so often that more and more of their manga books are being shrink-wrapped or covered in sealed plastic so that readers have to buy them before they can read them.

Manga is now one of the hottest publishing and pop culture phenomena, not just in Japan, where it originated, but now in North America, too. Where once the science fiction aisle ended, there are now several more shelving units devoted exclusively to manga, the Japanese comics that are growing so fast that most bookstores struggle to find enough room for the huge number of titles and series.

Manga has been part of Japanese culture for far longer than in North America. It began more than a century ago there, while it has only been available in America for approximately two decades. In that short period of time, however, manga has exploded in the American public. There are now numerous American manga publishers, such as Tokyopop and Seven Seas Entertainment, and manga divisions within general publishing houses, like Random House and HarperCollins. A new type of literature has arrived, graphic and dynamic but with substantial, complex narratives. These aren't your grandparent's comic books!

Manga Wall to Wall and Cover to Cover

Y ou can learn a lot about manga just by standing in the bookstore's aisle, looking at a few copies of the books, and watching other readers pore through issues. For example:

- The books are put in alphabetical order by title, not by author as with other fiction.
- Most series are at least several volumes long and can run to twenty, thirty, or more volumes.
- Most aisles are full of young people who read the books while standing up. Why? They can read them quickly and can complete a half dozen volumes in a short time. Plus, the content is so exciting and engaging, why bother sitting down?
- Manga comes in all kinds of styles, from romance, comedy, and drama to horror, science fiction, and sports. It is also tailored to readers of all ages, from preschoolers to grandparents and everyone in between.

The bright colors and large graphics of manga attract readers of all ages to see what kind of story is inside.

Another thing you will notice—if you aren't already a big fan—is that these books are extremely popular. There are usually multiple displays of new titles and new series found at the ends of shelving units and on new-release tables. Next to them are manga tie-in products like plastic figurines, T-shirts, posters, and even dolls. There is clearly no end in sight for how much consumer interest and enthusiasm these manga series can generate.

Types of Manga

Would you believe that there are more than a dozen kinds of manga? It's true! Here are the most popular kinds:

- **Kodomo manga:** for little kids
- **Shonen manga:** for teenage boys, dealing with action, battle, sports, science fiction, and fantasy
- **Shojo manga:** for teenage girls, dealing with romance, comedy, and drama
- **Seijin manga:** for adult men, dealing with business, crime, political drama, history, and military adventures
- **Redikomi manga:** for adult women, dealing with work, family, and romance
- **Gekiga manga:** on serious topics for adults
- **Doujinshi manga:** written by amateurs
- **Yonkoma manga:** traditional four-panel comic strips like those found in daily newspapers

Manga Rating System

Although each publishing company has different standards for rating its books, some of them have general rules to guide readers, just like Hollywood movies do (**G**=general public, **PG**=parental guidance, **PG13**=children over 13, **R**=age 18 and up, and **X**=age 21 and up), as well as video games

(**EC**=early childhood, **E**=everyone, **E10+**=everyone 10+, **T**=teen, **M**=mature 17+). Since Japan's ideas of what is appropriate regarding nudity, violence, language, and humor are often different from those in the United States, it is important to check the front of the book to see what rating it might carry. Here is what each one means:

A, Y, Youth, 7+, 10+ Acceptable for most ages, like a G- or PG-rated movie.

T, Teen, For ages 13+ Similar to a PG or PG-13 movie; may include some profanity, sexual references, or sexual humor.

T+, OT, Older Teen This is for older readers, akin to a PG-13 or R-rated movie; may include profanity, graphic violence, sex, or themes involving drugs and suicide.

M, Mature Audiences This is for adults and is akin to a R- or even X-rated movie; may contain graphic violence, explicit sex, or extremely strong language and very adult themes.

Can You Spot the Differences?

So, how do regular American comic books and Japanese manga differ? If you ask hardcore manga fans, don't be surprised if they gasp and then roll their eyes at you, seemingly embarrassed and offended by your ignorance. To them, the differences are so profound, so huge, and so numerous that they cannot imagine how you could possibly miss them. It

The Differences Between Manga and American Comics

Manga	American Comics
Printed almost entirely in black and white except for an occasional color story at the beginning	Printed in full color
Weekly magazine printed on recycled paper	Printed on high-cost paper for covers and interiors
First published in weekly/monthly magazines before being compiled into a thick book form	Typically published as stand-alone issues
Magazines released on a weekly basis, and they absolutely, positively never miss a single deadline	Publishers try to release their titles on a regular monthly basis but often miss deadlines
Can be purchased at many places, including newsstands, bookstores, candy shops, gift shops, train stations, etc.	Only found at certain book-stores or comic book shops; very difficult to order from catalogs

Read from right to left	Read from left to right
Written and illustrated by one person	Written and illustrated by a team
Have a summary of the story line printed on the back of the book	Have only the name of the comic on the front and usually an ad on the back
Thick, 200 pages, paperback-book size	Thin, 22 pages, 6.625" x 10.25" size

would be a little like asking what the difference between punk and opera is. They may both qualify as music, but that is where the similarity ends.

Why is manga so incredibly popular with readers of all ages? Some of the biggest fans say that it is because, unlike American comics that just repeat stories with the same superheroes over and over with little actual change, manga series have a clear and definite beginning, middle, and end. They tell a story with closure. They come to an end. Jason Thompson, author of *Manga: The Complete Guide*, compares a manga series to a popular, long-running television or cable series. The first book is like the pilot episode. Each story is like a weekly episode, and when the final volume is written, it brings the entire story to an end like a series finale.

The art found in different manga series is dramatic and unique. It works to speed the story along.

Although each manga story is unique, the casts of manga characters tend to be fairly consistent. Most story lines include a main character, a funny sidekick, a single and usually very attractive female character, and a wise old man. Of course, the villains typically include a charming but evil leader and a strong but perhaps dim-witted and nasty henchman.

Censorship

As many parents have accidentally discovered, some manga books are a lot racier than those of the old *Archie* comics days, when Archie was always trying to decide whether to date Betty or Veronica. Superman used to worship Lois Lane from afar, but manga characters engage in much more explicit behavior and activities. In fact, in the early 1990s in the United Kingdom, some explicit series of manga were pulled from the shelves and labeled as pornography. That is why many of the series have started putting labels on the covers to direct readers to age-appropriate types of stories. Some also include parental advisory stickers.

In Japan, censorship is not quite the same as it is in the United States. Japanese publishers will often include more sex and violence than American publishers will in books kids and teens are likely to read. When books are translated from Japanese to English, one part of the American editor's job might be to cut some of the material that could be considered offensive by some. Examples include:

- Detailed sexual scenes
- Overly gory violence
- Cruelty to animals
- Racist images
- Drug references
- Unauthorized drawings of name-brand products
- Smoking by underage characters

Not all American manga publishers remove this material, of course. It is an individual decision. Publishers do not want to offend readers, but they also do not want to water down the stories so much that readers are disappointed. If you are not sure if your favorite series are edited like this, consider where you bought the books. If they were purchased at Wal-Mart or other large department stores or ordered through Scholastic, chances are they were edited and censored. Those found on the shelves in comic stores and national bookstore chains, like Borders and Barnes & Noble, are usually unedited.

Why do Japanese manga artists and publishers include some of these elements in their stories? In some cases, the reason is the differences between Japanese and American culture. For example, Japan has a very low crime rate. When manga artists depict violent scenes, it is often drawn from their imaginations, not ripped from the latest news headlines. They aren't mirroring their society so much as depicting a darker, more nightmarish funhouse version of it. In the United States, violence is often an everyday reality, and manga creators would run the risk of

Some Manga Facts

- The biggest-selling manga weekly so far is *Shonen Jump*. It sold over six million copies in one week.
- How long are some manga series? *Dragon Ball/Dragon Ball Z* was forty-two volumes long. *Ranma* was thirty-eight volumes long.
- In 2006, the longest-running manga series in history published its 150th issue. Its title is *Kochira Katsushika-Ku Kameari Koen-mae Hashutsujo*, which, in Japanese, means *This Is the Police Station in Front of Kamerari Park in Katsushika-Ku Ward*.
- Manga magazines are often up to nine hundred pages long and are made up of multiple single episodes. In Japan, they are called "phone books."
- An overwhelming 40 percent of all publications sold in Japan are manga.
- In the United States, the manga business earns $180 million each year. In Japan, manga publishing brings in $4.7 billion annually.
- More than forty syndicated newspapers throughout the United States now carry a few pages of manga in addition to their colorful traditional Sunday comics.

offending the sensibilities of those affected by it or of being accused of capitalizing on real crime and suffering.

So . . . What Is It About?

If you ask what manga is about, be prepared for a big sigh. It is about . . . everything. As Tokyopop publisher Mike Kiley said in an article called "Manga Nobel Prize," "There are manga that are full of big-eyed girls and robots, there are manga that tell the story of professional golfers, there are cooking manga, there are manga that are very sort of indie and western in flavor. It's a very broad palate and kind of difficult to generalize . . . There are manga produced for 3-year-olds and there are manga that are written for 80-year-olds."

The Job Market

Manga is so hot today that the job market surrounding it is exploding. In Japan, *manga-ka*, or manga artists, are treated like celebrities. They are revered much like movie stars are in the United States. In Japan, people line up to catch a glimpse of these artists. Fans ask for their autographs. Paparazzi, those rabid photographers who chase down celebrities, hound manga artists for candid shots every bit as intensely as they pursue Angelina Jolie, Brad Pitt, and Britney Spears.

With the number of fans soaring, major manga publishers like Kodansha, Tokyopop, and Seven Seas Entertainment (which all publish English-language manga) are always soliciting and reviewing work from new artists who want to break into the market. They are searching primarily for signs of talent and creativity. This book will give you the inside look at the world of manga and how to enter into it as an artist, an assistant, a translator, or several other positions crucial to the manga creation, production, and marketing process. It also includes helpful information on what materials you will need, the contacts you can make, and the jobs you might hold.

Japanese manga artists are often asked for their autographs. Here, Natsuki Takaya, creator of the *Fruits Basket* series, signs books for fans at a book fair held in Germany in 2007.

A Brief History of Manga

The word "manga" was first used in the 1800s by a Japanese artist named Katsushika Hokusai. He used to fill up all of his notebooks with sketches, doodles, and drawings. He was not sure what to call these little pictures but finally came up with the word "manga." During his lifetime, he created tens of thousands of prints, paintings, and other illustrations. Most of them were of Japanese landscapes and seascapes, like crashing waves and mountain thunderstorms.

So, what does the word "manga" mean anyway? It has been translated in a number of different ways, with each translation providing one part of the total picture that is manga:

- Entertaining visuals
- Whimsical sketches
- Lighthearted pictures
- Involuntary sketches
- Irresponsible pictures

Katsushika Hokusai's famous painting *The Great Wave of Kanagawa* was part of a series he drew called *Thirty-Six Views of Mount Fuji.*

The Father of Modern Manga

The first real manga comics to come out of Japan were drawn in a European style. Later, they were drawn in four-panel comic style, like the comic strips that still appear daily in America's newspapers. In 1931, a comic called *The Four Immigrants* was published in San Francisco. It was drawn by an artist named Henry Yoshitaka Kiyama. He was living in California while studying Western art, and his manga told the story of people who came to America in search of their dreams. It was

The Four Immigrants Manga

A Japanese Experience in San Francisco, 1904–1924

by Henry (Yoshitaka) Kiyama
Translated, with an introduction and notes, by Frederik L. Schodt

From servants in fancy homes to workers in the fields,
through earthquakes, riots, a World's Fair, war, and Prohibition —
the true story of four young Japanese men who pursued their
dreams in the rough and tumble of American history

The Four Immigrants was made up of fifty-two episodes and focused on the lives of Kiyama and three of his friends. It took place in San Francisco during the years 1904 to 1924.

the first time this fairly typical immigrant "coming to America" story had been presented from a Japanese perspective.

During World War II, the Japanese were far too busy fighting to have time to draw "whimsical sketches," but once the war was over, the art of manga came back with a vengeance. It had a lot of American "flavor" built into it now because the two cultures had mixed so much during the war despite fighting on opposite sides. American soldiers had brought comics with them overseas, and American cartoons had been shown to the Japanese. The artistic and narrative ideas in them began to inspire manga artists.

The Japanese public loved this new art form that was emerging. It was both affordable and accessible. The biggest manga artist of the day was Osamu Tezuka, the man who would come to be known as the father of modern manga. He was the creator of the long-running series *Astro Boy*, a story about a young boy who happens to also be a super-powered robot.

Tezuka's day job was as a factory worker. He had seen and greatly admired Walt Disney's drawings of Mickey Mouse and Donald Duck. He became inspired to create his own drawn characters. He wanted them to have personalities and styles that would bring them to life. He wanted people to remember, recognize, and love them like they did Mickey and Donald.

Tezuka was the first artist to go beyond drawing simple comic strips or single pictures and instead made a novel-length drawn story. Published in 1947, the book *Treasure*

During the 2006 Tezuka: The Marvel of Manga exhibition in Melbourne's National Gallery of Victoria, Astro Boy wanders by to check out some of the stories written about him. The Australian exhibition featured over 150,000 pages of manga and 700 different titles.

Island was two hundred pages long and sold an astonishing four hundred thousand copies. It was the story of a young boy and a pirate who went in search of treasure together. Tezuka was the first artist to use the unique drawing style of zooming in and panning out on characters in emulation of the camera techniques used in movies. While this technique is a common one today, when Tezuka did it, it was startlingly new and daring. It grabbed the readers' attention. It also inspired other artists to follow in his footsteps and gave birth to the art of manga.

Manga's Ups and Downs

By the end of the 1950s, manga had grown enough that its characters and stories were being adapted for anime (Japanese animation), toys, and feature-length movies. As time went by, more types of manga were being written for audiences of different ages and interests. The business just kept growing as did the fan communities, or *otaku*, that formed around it. Many people began drawing their own stories at home, based on the famous characters of popular series. These homemade and self-published stories were known as *doujinshi*.

The Manga Museum

Want to know of one place where you can see far more manga than you can at your local comic shop? The International Manga Museum in Kyoto, Japan, which opened in 2007, had more than ten thousand visitors in its first two weeks. By the end of 2008, the museum plans to have more than three hundred thousand pieces of manga on display and in its archives.

The boys' magazine *Shonen Jump* was first published in the late 1970s and sold millions of new issues each week. In the 1990s, the manga business took a severe nosedive in Japan as the economy struggled and the Internet was introduced, which offered stiff competition in attracting and keeping the attention of young Japanese. People still read their favorite series, but now it was done more through *mawashiyomi*, or borrowing

This English-language version of the popular *Shonen Jump* first hit American newsstands in autumn 2002. This copy features a full-color drawing of Yu-gi-oh, one of manga's most popular characters.

copies from friends. Manga sales dropped quickly. It took several years for them to climb again, but then they once again soared.

Coming to America

The first manga book to be translated from Japanese to English was Kazuo Koike's *Lone Wolf and Cub* in 1987. It told the story of Ogami Itto, a warrior who was falsely accused and forced to become an assassin. Together, with his three-year-old son, Daigoro—the cub of the books' title—Ogami Itto traveled around seeking revenge.

Europe, Asia, and Latin America were far ahead in the manga game. They had been reading it for years before the books finally made their way to the United States. Americans quickly made up for lost time, however. They gobbled up the new type of comic as fast as they could and almost instantly created an industry that had been unheard of just a few months earlier. By 2007, more

And the Winner Is . . .

Since 1971, the Tezuka Award has been handed out twice a year by the Japanese publisher Shueisha. It is given to new artists that show the most promise. Top prize is one million Japanese yen, or about $9,000 (as of December 2007). In August 2007, the first International Manga Awards were presented. As quoted in the article "Exploring the History of Manga," the Japanese minister for foreign affairs stated, "Japan is the birthplace of manga, and I would like to give young manga creators from around the world a prestigious award from Japan."

Almost 150 people sent in their samples, which were evaluated by four professional manga artists. The winner was Lee Chi Ching from Hong Kong for his manga *Sun Zi's Tactics*.

than one thousand manga series had been translated into English. Bookstores were forced to add more shelving just to accommodate all these manga titles.

The *Lone Wolf and Cub* series was quickly followed by the translation of several other series, including *Area 88*, about a young pilot's adventures in a secluded air force base; *Mai the Psychic Girl*, focusing on a fourteen-year-old girl who has amazing psychic abilities; and *The Legend of Kamui*, which is set in feudal Japan and explores the topic of discrimination.

In the mid-1990s, American comic book sales actually began to drop and manga sales began to rise. The main audience for these books was boys, but that all changed for good in 1995 with the arrival of a group of short-skirted, long-legged, big-eyed, magical girls named after planets. Their adventures were the basis for the stories of *Sailor Moon*, written and illustrated by female manga-ka Naoko Takeuchi. Suddenly, manga had girls clamoring for more stories and more anime adaptations and TV episodes. *Shojo*, or manga specifically written for girls, had arrived in the United States.

In 2002, the American manga market got even bigger when two Japanese publishers launched in the United States. One of them published the weekly *Raijin Comics*, while the other created an English version of the ever-popular *Shonen Jump*. They were followed by more and more companies. Manga had made it to American shores, and it was there to stay. In fact, it was set to take over the comic marketplace.

A Familiar Name

Glancing down the manga aisle, does one publisher's name tend to keep popping up? Most likely it is Tokyopop, an American manga publisher and one of the most influential companies in the industry. The biggest publishers of manga are all located in Tokyo, Japan: Kodansha, Shueisha, Shogakukan, and Hakusensha. Yet the homegrown Tokyopop has become a major force within the business and dominates the American market.

It all began when a young American "geek" named Stu Levy took a trip to Japan. A long-time fan of video games and the

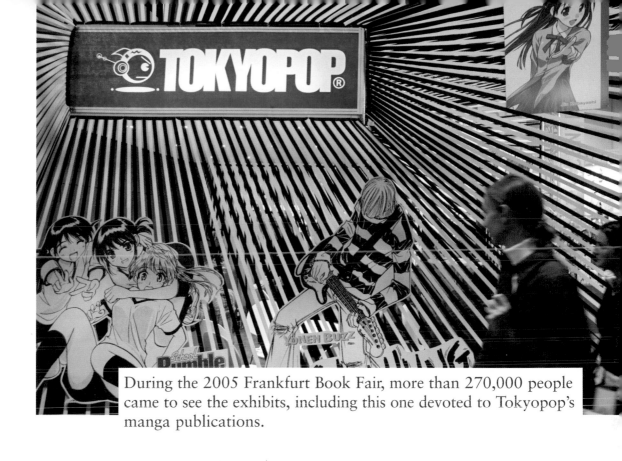

During the 2005 Frankfurt Book Fair, more than 270,000 people came to see the exhibits, including this one devoted to Tokyopop's manga publications.

role-playing game Dungeons and Dragons, he adored Japan, immersing himself completely in its culture, especially its pop culture. In 1997, Levy founded *Mixx* magazine, which quickly became renamed *Tokyopop*. A mere ten years later, the company is the largest U.S.-owned creator of manga. Ignoring the advice of others in the business, Levy kept the original right-to-left reading format in his series—and it worked. "Tokyopop created what is known as the authentic Japanese manga," Calvin Reid, coeditor of trade magazine *PW Comics Week,* told *Time* magazine. He was also behind the move to change the book's shape to the size of a paperback and stick to an affordable $9.99 per issue price. Future plans include a partnership with Sony to produce a series of motion pictures based on some of Tokyopop's most popular manga characters.

In response to critics who say that Americans can't produce authentic manga, Stu Levy, now the CEO of Tokyopop, told *Time* magazine, "Manga is like hip-hop. It's a lifestyle. To say that you can't draw it because you don't have the DNA is just silly."

Leading Manga Artists

Y ou've been learning all about manga's history and how the business works. Now let's put it all together and take a quick look at some of the most respected names in the business. These are some of the authors/artists you see filling the manga shelves in the bookstore. How did they get started and where are they going next?

Drawing What He Sees and Knows

When Akira Toriyama was little, he did a lot of drawing in school. The habit kept growing, and soon, as he put it in an interview with DragonBallMaster.com, "I started to draw portraits of friends and whatnot and started to think drawing was fun." Watching a lot of TV shows and movies changed how he drew. He was a huge fan of *Astro Boy* cartoons on television, as well as Disney classics like *101 Dalmatians*.

The first popular character he developed was a little robot girl and the family of inventors with whom she lived. The

The character of Dragon Ball Z is one of the most familiar in all of manga. His image is found in books and movies and on clothing.

series was known as *Dr. Slump.* Toriyama was not sure where to go from there. "I always liked Jackie Chan and had seen his *Drunken Master II* many times. [My editor] encouraged me to draw a kung fu manga if I liked it that much," he said in the interview. That character turned out to be Dragon Boy, and the series *Dragon Ball* was born. It was a huge hit and has generated more than three billion dollars in sales of books, movies, toys, clothing, and other products. In 1986, it became a television series. Toriyama did not have creative control over this show, however, and instead stood on the sidelines, making only occasional comments or editorial directions. "I don't tend

A Nobel Prize In . . . Manga?

Manga may be great, but does it truly qualify for a Nobel Prize? Apparently the Japanese government thinks so. In 2007, it announced that it will award a Nobel Prize of Manga to comic book artists living outside of Japan who "best contribute to the worldwide spread of the art form." According to Alexandra Munroe in a story for Fox News, "Official forces within Japanese government are recognizing the leadership that Japan has in the world in this area of cultural production. And they do. No one comes close. They realize it's their Hollywood." The idea for this prize came from Foreign Minister Taro Aso, a huge manga fan who strongly believes in the power of pop culture to influence and inspire the public.

to interfere with the animator's process," he explained in the interview. "I wanted a fantastic story, so I did tell them that, but the basic production was all up to them."

Much of what Toriyama writes is based on what he sees around him. "It's been a habit of mine since childhood to always be looking around," he said. "For my work, the town scenery, small things, and people's clothes all are useful." Instead of simply drawing what he sees at the time, Toriyama "burns it into [his] vision." This way he can remember it later when he needs it and simply sketch it in. "I can probably draw most anything that way," he added.

Sailing to Success

When Naoko Takeuchi got dressed in her sailor suit and headed for classes at her high school, she probably never dreamed that her name would one day be known all over the world for writing about young girls whose trademark was dressing just like her—in sailor suits. After getting her college degree in chemistry and becoming a licensed pharmacist, the notion of a successful career in manga must have seemed even more improbable and remote. Today, however, as the creator of the eighteen-volume *Sailor Moon* series and tie-in television shows and movies, she is one of the brightest stars in the manga universe.

When Takeuchi was nineteen, she began working for the publishing company Kodansha. She got the job by placing second in the Nakayoshi Comic Prize for Newcomers contest with her series called *Love Call*. Next, she wrote a manga version of the American classic novel *Daddy Long Legs* by Jean Webster, about a college student who is supported by an unknown and unseen benefactor. After next creating a series about figure skating called *The Cherry Project*, she began her *Sailor Moon* books. Her female characters, Sailor Moon, Mars, Mercury, Jupiter, and Venus, put on very short sailor suits and went throughout the universe righting wrongs.

Blending work, pleasure, and romance in 1999, Takeuchi married fellow manga artist Yoshihiro Togashi, creator of the

Yu Yu Hakusho series. Together, they are Mom and Dad to a little boy.

The Mothers of Manga

Have you spotted the name "Clamp" on some of the manga series you've been perusing? It may not sound like the name of a group of female manga creators, but it is. Clamp is made up of four Japanese women: Satsuki Igarashi, Apapa Mokona, Tsubaki Nekoi, and Ageha Ohkawa. The group began with eleven members but slowly shrank down to the four that are left. They are responsible for creating

The characters Inu-yasha and Kagome *(above)*, created by Rumiko Takahashi, are known in Japan and the United States.

more than twenty extremely popular manga series, many of which have been turned into equally successful movies. Dallas Middaugh, associate publisher of the Del Rey Manga division of Random House, recently stated in an article for the *New York Times*, "Clamp have been an integral part of the manga

As time has passed, more and more girls have found manga series that they enjoy. The books produced by the Clamp team, like the one being read above, appeal to many young people.

explosion that's occurred in the U.S. over the past several years. Their fluid, dramatic artwork and storytelling style struck a strong chord with male and female manga readers."

Some of Clamp's most popular series include *Chobits*, *xxxHOLIC*, and *Cardcaptor Sakura*. *Chobits* is a science fiction comedy centering on a nerdy student and a beautiful android. In *xxxHOLIC*, a psychic high school boy meets a talented sorceress who is able to grant anyone's wish. *Cardcaptor Sakura* is about a fourth-grade girl who finds a deck of enchanted cards and then has many supernatural experiences as she tries to prevent the cards from wreaking havoc in the world. Her best friend, Tomoyo, makes her special costumes to wear as she embarks on each new adventure. "It's common in girls' manga for a character to transform, as Sailor Moon does, and we wanted to incorporate that into *Sakura*," Ageha Ohkawa told the *New York Times*. "But many [female manga characters] always wear the same outfit, so we wanted to add a twist. We feel it's pretty sad for a girl to wear the same outfit all the time."

Each one of the women in Clamp plays a different role within the group, with Ohkawa in charge. "I decide who does the characters, and what she's going to do with them, as a director would pick his actors," she explained to the *Times*. "I assign the roles, depending on the genre of the series: horror, comedy, and so forth. I also choose the visual style." The results include some of the most popular manga titles, not just in Japan but worldwide.

Not For or By Men Only

Manga for girls may seem new to Americans, but it is not new in Japan. One of the first manga series to develop after World War II was female artist Machiko Hasegawa's series *Sazae-san*, featuring the female protagonist Sazae Fuguta. It ran from 1946 to 1974 and was read by almost all Japanese, regardless of age or gender.

Hasegawa's series was followed in 1969 by one produced by a group of female manga artists who called themselves the Magnificent 24s. The women produced the popular series *The Rose of Versailles*, a story of a cross-dressing woman who pretended to be a captain in pre-revolutionary France.

Riding the Waves

One of the hottest manga series on the market today is *One Piece*, created by Eiichiro Oda. All artists are inspired by something. In Oda's case, it was seafaring, marauding Vikings. By seventeen, he had already won several awards for his work, including the coveted Tezuka Award. He worked as an assistant on the well-known series *Rurouni Kenshin* and then won another award, the Hop Step. In 1997, he created the first installment of *One Piece*, and it was a huge hit immediately.

One Piece is about a teenager named Monkey D. Luffy who is trying to become the King of Pirates and search out One Piece, a lost treasure. He has a special power—he can stretch like rubber. But he also operates under a tragic curse—he cannot swim, a definite problem for someone who spends most of his time out at sea. Although no one in the book dies, the series is known for its intense and bloody fight scenes.

Other Leading Artists

There are many other important names in manga, of course. Some important artists and manga titles to check out include the following:

Name	Information
Shotaro Ishinomori	Former assistant on *Astro Boy*, he created *The Legend of Zelda*
Ashura Itoh/Benimaru Itoh	Creator of the popular *Pokemon: Pikachu Meets the Press*
Go Nagai	Manga-ka of the popular *Devilman* and *Mazinger* series
Masamune Shirow	The person behind the *Ghost in the Shell* series
Rumiko Takahashi	Creator of the Inu-yasha and *Ranma 1/2* series

The work of each one of these manga-ka can be enthralling to read, dazzling to the eye, and very educational if you are looking for a career in manga, especially as an artist and creator. Learn from the best and study their work. You'll have a lot of fun doing so. Research has never been so entertaining!

Breaking into the Business

In Japan, almost everyone wants to be a manga-ka. Most manga publishers, including the growing number of American publishers of manga, are swamped with artist applications. Sometimes, they are so overwhelmed with people sending in their portfolios that they hold their own talent contests to a select few. Hundreds of people show up to try out. The winner often gets his or her manga story published in a special edition of the publisher's magazine, as well as a job offer.

Some manga artists do not want to wait until they are chosen by a publisher, so they pay to have their work published and then sell it themselves. This type of manga is called *doujinshi*. It is not unusual for some of these self-published stories to be picked up later by companies and printed professionally.

Artists and Editors

Once a manga-ka has been hired by a new company, he or she is given an editor to work with. The editor is like a guide.

He or she oversees the artist's work, giving advice, tips, ideas, and suggestions on ways to make the stories easy to sell to eager readers like you. The editor also helps develop the story's plot and fine-tune the characters' personalities. Japanese manga artists have great job security. It is almost unheard of for an artist to be hired and then fired. The editor just keeps working one-on-one with the artist until he or she finds his or her particular path to success.

It takes a lot of time, hard work, imagination, and skill to be a manga-ka. They are responsible for almost every detail of a story. They come up with the story ideas. They write all of the words. They draw the characters and come up with their expressions. It is a great deal of work. In a typical workweek, they are expected to draw twenty entire pages. That means between eighty and one hundred pages of drawing every single month. It can be grueling, and the artists sacrifice a lot of sleep in the early years of their careers, as they work around the clock to get those twenty pages done each week.

Assistants and Interns

Many manga artists are given several assistants to help them get their work done. These can be paid assistants or unpaid interns. Some of these assistants may be personal friends. Others may be family or just would-be artists hoping to get their feet in the door of a manga publishing house one way or another.

The Japanese animators shown here are drawing images for an upcoming anime (animated film) production.

Assistants have many different jobs, from being "gofers" who run errands ranging from picking up new art supplies or grabbing a cup of coffee to helping out with the drawings by laying down the screen tone (a series of black-and-white dots that form background patterns), gathering reference materials, drawing backgrounds and crowd scenes, and helping to do any of the inking or computer effects.

Positions Available in Manga Publishing

If you want to be part of the manga world, there are many different ways to get started. You may picture yourself as a hot manga-ka with crowds of screaming kids lined up calling out your name and asking for your autograph, as you sketch the most incredible manga story ever written. This may be possible, but there are a lot of other steps you need to go through first.

One of the most important first steps is learning the different positions you can have within a manga company. These can include:

- Pencillers
- Inkers
- Toners
- Assistants
- Translators
- Writers/artists

Penciller

Purpose: This person is the head of the visual team. It is this job that truly controls the overall look of the entire project. The most important key to a successful manga story is called visual pacing, interspersing slower moments and dialogue with more dynamic, action-packed panels.

Required Skills: You must have a strong knowledge of manga and how it typically appears. Without the help of words, a person should be able to look at your penciled sketches and immediately understand what is going on, what emotions the character is feeling, and so on. You have to be able to draw the backgrounds in complete perspective, while also drawing humans that follow the general rule of physics: characters should only move in ways that are anatomically possible. You also have to be able to convey a huge range of emotions just through facial expressions. Can you make a demon look silly? A teenager look suspicious? A wizard look confused? A small child look disappointed? You'd better. If you can't do any of these things, keep practicing.

Inker

Purpose: Using brushes, markers, and pens, this person is in charge of bringing depth and shadows to drawings.

Required Skills: You must be able to understand line weight and how to use it. Line weight is the heaviness, darkness, and strength of a line. The line weight you use for various characters and objects determines a lot about their meaning, action, mood, strength, and personality.

Toner

Purpose: This person provides depth and texture to line art. The process often involves using computer software like PhotoShop, Drawing Tablet, CorelDRAW, CG Illust, and Comicworks.

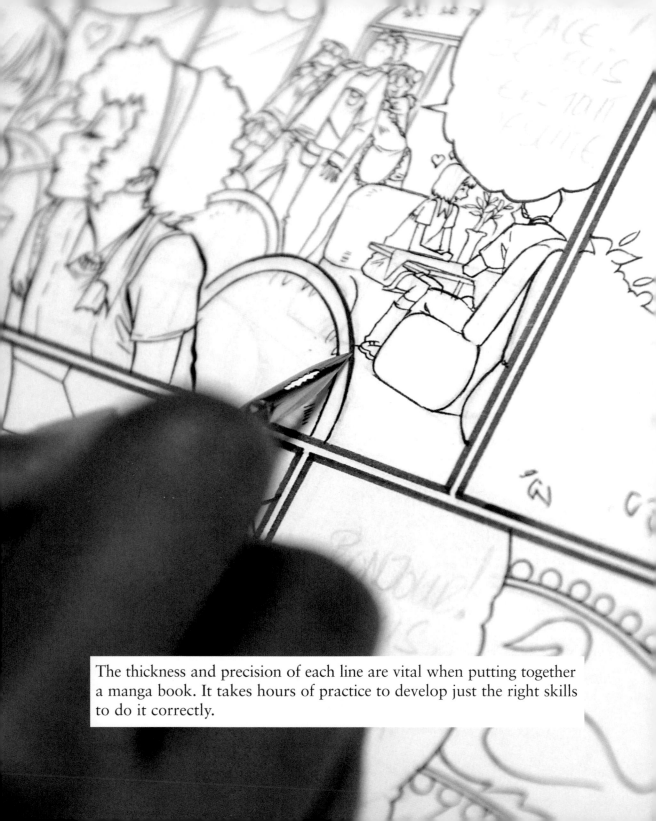

The thickness and precision of each line are vital when putting together a manga book. It takes hours of practice to develop just the right skills to do it correctly.

Required Skills: You must know how to use digital screen toning and digital grayscale coloring. A good toner has to be able to work well with the inker and penciller because it takes a team effort to produce the finished drawings.

Assistant

Purpose: To perform whatever jobs the main artist requests.
Required Skills: Patience and willingness to do what is needed, and strong artistic skills and familiarity with manga, since you will often be asked to do pencil and ink backgrounds, fill in shaded areas, and draw borders.

Translator

Purpose: To translate Japanese manga series into English and other languages, since many series are distributed and sold internationally.
Required Skills: Extreme fluency in Japanese and in whatever language you are translating the work into; strong familiarity with the different censorship rules of the individual company, the country the work will be sold in, and the stores carrying the manga line; and familiarity with slang terms of both languages to ensure they are translated correctly.

Writer/Artist

Purpose: To be the creator of a manga series from start to finish—the story, the characters, the illustrations.

The variety of manga titles available grows every day. There are now stories to appeal to readers of any age and both genders.

Required Skills: Typically, you will need to submit material to the publishing company in a portfolio. Make sure to send in copies only, not originals. Here is what the portfolio should generally include (but remember, each company has it own submissions rules, so carefully follow their guidelines):

- Four to six sequential pages from your story; make sure they are fully inked, toned, and lettered before sending.
- A one-page synopsis of your story, including what you will do in the first three volumes, a summary of the main character's journey, and the bad guy's motivations.

- One page of character descriptions: personalities, appearances, names, clothing, quirks, where they have been and where they are going within the story line.
- Full-page illustrations of the three main characters.
- Marketing information: Who is the intended audience for this series? What other series is it similar to? What makes this series special or unique?

Knowing the different roles involved with working in manga is essential. You never know where you might get your foot in the door and where that foot may lead you!

Becoming a Manga-Ka

You want to be manga-ka, so what can you do to get started? There are a lot of steps you can take right now. Let's go over them and then take a look at the kind of materials you may need to purchase as you develop your ability as a manga artist.

Draw often. This seems like a given, but it is the most important step. Make a point of drawing on a regular basis, not just when you are bored and have some time to kill. Drawing is like piano playing; you need to practice every day to grow in ability and keep your skills sharp. If you make drawing a part of your daily routine, then later, if you get a job in the business, it will already seem routine to work on it regularly.

Learn new skills wherever and whenever you can. Never pass up a chance to expand your drawing skills. If there is a workshop at your school, go to it. If there is a community college class, enroll in it. If you have a friend who is a great artist, ask him or her to tutor you. If your art teacher at school is willing to give you extra time, take it. If you have an art center in your city, visit it and see what it has to offer you. You can even consider taking an online class—just make sure it is a legitimate one and not one whose only goal is to take your money and provide little or no skilled and professional instruction.

Attend conferences or conventions. If there are any art, manga, or anime gatherings in your area, attend them. You will not only get a great education and terrific free samples of materials, you will be given the chance to network with others who are doing what you are doing and perhaps meet people who can help you connect to other opportunities.

Look for internships. If you are lucky enough to have a manga publishing company in your area, see if you can get an internship there. The information you learn and the connections you make will be absolutely invaluable. Consider applying for a job at your local comic store or bookstore. Manga artists and publishing representatives pass through these stores regularly for promotional tours, providing you with a great opportunity to network and

Each manga artist has a unique way of creating characters. Many artists' drawings are so colorful and detailed that they can be considered art as well as entertainment.

discuss their work, your work, and strategies for breaking into the business. You can also get more plugged into the whole manga community, both on the consumer and producer/creative end.

Spend time online. Go onto the blogs and the manga forums and see what others are doing and saying. Ask questions there. Look up the resources others use or mention.

Fans attend a Chara Fes, or character festival. They often come
to events in full costume to look like their favorite characters from
manga series, computer games, and anime.

Show your art to others for feedback. You need to hear the
opinions, comments, and thoughts of others about your
art. Seek the opinions of manga fans because they will
know what to look for in your drawings.

Finding Job Listings

Where can you go to look for manga jobs? Where do you go for
almost everything else in the world that you need? Online, of

MangaNEXT

In 2006, the first American-based manga convention was held in Secaucus, New Jersey. Called MangaNEXT, it attracted thousands to the area. "With the growth of the manga market outpacing the anime market today, we felt it was an appropriate time to introduce a manga convention," said Eugene Cheng, former chairman of AnimeNEXT, a Japanese animation convention. The convention has now become an annual event.

course. Just like with most types of jobs, manga has its own job boards where different companies list their needs for employees.

First, start with the home pages of some of your favorite manga publishers. They often have a job board or a page where they list openings, as well as their submission policies. You may have to search, but they are there. Next, go on Google, Monster.com, or CareerBuilder.com and type "manga jobs" and "manga job boards" in the search box. Often this will lead you to specific job listings or related sites.

Making a Good Impression

If you are going after a job in manga, you are going to be up against some pretty intense competition, so you have to really

Cutting-Edge Test Prep

"The colossal villain scampered after the inconsequential heroine just in time to observe her clandestine meeting." Huh?

The test prep company Kaplan and U.S. manga publisher Tokyopop have joined together to give you manga entertainment along with your vocabulary test prep. The stories and art are pure manga, but in the midst of all the action, some hefty vocabulary words are thrown at you. Learn them as you read, and, hopefully, you will do better on your PSAT, SAT, or ACT.

do your homework. If you come across as unprofessional, amateurish, or lazy, you aren't going to make the impression you want to and someone else will get the job you want so badly. You can kill your chances of getting hired before they even look at your first piece of art. It is important to arrive for an interview early and well-dressed. Have a resume and samples of your work readily available and neatly organized and presented. Come prepared by researching the company ahead of time. Know exactly what series they publish, which artists are in their stable, and what their company history is.

How you approach the job search process depends greatly on what position you are going to apply for. Although there are people who are willing to take most positions, the role of artist is usually the most highly desired one of all. You may have to start as an intern or an assistant and pay your dues for a few years by helping inkers, toners, pencillers, editors, and artists with their jobs. But you will be in the thick of the action, with access to people who can look at your work, offer suggestions for improvement, and possibly publish it one day. You may be able to work up the ranks until you become a series creator yourself.

However you become a manga artist, either by patiently working up the ladder of a publishing house or by submitting your work and having it accepted, it will all start with your portfolio. A portfolio is a way to put all of your work together into one place so that publishers can see it. It concentrates the best work you have into one convenient, easily browsed location.

Putting Together an Art Portfolio

You can find many different sizes of professional portfolio cases in arts and crafts supply stores. These will allow you to put your best drawings in them without worrying about folding or creasing them in any way. You can also make your own portfolio. It takes time but often costs a lot less

Hinako Takanaga, a Japanese manga artist, smiles as she holds up a copy of her book for photographers to see at a book fair in Germany in 2007.

than what you pay in the store. Be sure to remember never to turn in your original drawings when applying for a job. They are far too valuable. Pay to have high-quality copies made and keep your originals someplace very safe. You may also be able to create a digital portfolio by scanning your work and burning it to disc or posting it to a Web site you've created.

Becoming a manga artist is not an easy goal, but in a world where the demand for manga just keeps growing, it is sure to be steady work. If you have the passion, the talent, and the dedication to pursue it, then go for it! Perhaps you can be one of those special people who spend their lives making those highly sought-after "whimsical sketches."

Glossary

censorship The cutting out or omission of material that is deemed offensive.

discrimination Unfair treatment of a person or group on the basis of prejudice.

doujinshi Self-published manga.

manga Japanese word that translates as "whimsical sketches"; Japanese comics and print cartoons.

manga-ka A manga artist.

otaku Fans.

pharmacist A person trained to prepare and give out drugs and medications.

screen tone A technique for applying textures and shadings to drawings.

sequential Occurring in a row or in consecutive order.

shojo Manga for girls.

shonen Manga for boys.

synopsis A brief summary of a lengthy text or story.

tachiyomi Japanese term for the practice of standing and reading.

For More Information

Kodansha International
Otowa YK Building
1-17-14 Otowa
Bunkyo-ku, Tokyo, Japan 112-8652
Web sites: http://www.kodanclub.com
http://www.kodansha-intl.com
> Kodansha is a privately owned publishing company that has been run by consecutive generations of the Noma family since 1909. It is a leader in Japanese book, magazine, and manga publishing.

The Kyoto International Museum of Manga
Karasuma-Oike, Nakagyo-ku
Kyoto, Japan
Web site: http://www.kyotomm.com/english/index.html
> The museum collects, preserves, and exhibits manga and animation materials for research and study purposes.

Tokyopop

People's Bank Building

5900 Wilshire Boulevard

Los Angeles, CA 90036-5020

(323) 692-6700

Web site: http://www.tokyopop.com

> Tokyopop has become an influential youth-oriented entertainment brand and the top innovator of manga creations.

VIZ Media, LLC

295 Bay Street

San Francisco, CA 94133

Web site: http://www.viz.com

> VIZ Media is a leader in the publishing and distribution of Japanese manga for English-speaking audiences in North America and a global licensor of Japanese animation.

Web Sites

Due to the changing nature of Internet links, Rosen Publishing has developed an online list of Web sites related to the subject of this book. This site is updated regularly. Please use this link to access the list:

http://www.rosenlinks.com/exc/maar

For Further Reading

Estudio Joso. *The Monster Book of Manga: Draw Like the Experts.* New York, NY: Collins Design, 2006.

Glass, Sherri, and Jim Wentzel. *Cool Careers for People Who Love Manga, Comics, and Animation.* New York, NY: Rosen Publishing, 2007.

Hodges, Jared. *Digital Manga Workshop: An Artist's Guide to Creating Manga Illustrations on Your Computer.* New York, NY: Collins Design, 2005.

Ikari Studio. *The Monster Book of More Manga: Draw Like the Experts.* New York, NY: Collins Design, 2007.

Lammers, Wayne. *Japanese the Manga Way: An Illustrated Guide to Grammar and Structure.* Berkeley, CA: Stone Bridge Press, 2004.

Layman, John. *The Complete Idiot's Guide to Drawing Manga, Illustrated.* New York, NY: Alpha Books, 2005.

Lewis, Bruce. *Draw Manga: How to Draw in Your Own Unique Style.* New York, NY: Collins & Brown, 2005.

Nagatomo, Haruno. *Draw Your Own Manga: All the Basics.* Tokyo, Japan: Kodansha International, 2003.

Bibliography

Albert, Aaron. "Manga 101: Basic Walk-Through of the Manga
World." About.com. Retrieved November 2007 (http://
comicbooks.about.com/od/manga/ss/manga101.htm).

AnimeInfo.org. "History of Manga." Retrieved November 2007
(http://www.animeinfo.org/animeu/hist102-l1.html).

Bonisteel, Sara. "Japan to Give 'Nobel Prize' for Foreign Comic-
Book Artists." FoxNews.com, May 22, 2007. Retrieved
December 2007 (http://www.foxnews.com/story/0,2933,
274673,00.html).

DragonBallMaster.com. "Akira Toriyama Interview." Retrieved
December 2007 (http://www.dragonballmaster.com/index.
php?id=fanfic/Fanstuff/interview.html).

Dummies.com. "Tracing the Rise of Manga's Popularity."
Retrieved November 2007 (http://www.dummies.com/
WileyCDA/DummiesArticle/id-5104.html).

Gravett, Paul. *Manga: 60 Years of Japanese Comics*. New York,
NY: Collins Design, 2004

Masters, Coco. "America Is Drawn to Manga." *Time*, August 10, 2006. Retrieved December 2007 (http://www.time.com/time/magazine/article/0,9171,1223355-1,00.html).

McLean, Thomas. "Manga Ready to Be Hollywood's Next Big Thing." VarietyAsiaOnline.com, October 26, 2007. Retrieved November 2007 (http://www.varietyasiaonline.com/content/view/4794/1).

Okabayashi, Kensuke. *Manga for Dummies*. New York, NY: For Dummies, 2007.

Rio. "Materials." Manga Tutorials. Retrieved November 2007 (http://www.mangatutorials.com/tut/materials.htm).

SliceofSciFi.com. "Manga Nobel Prize." May 2007. Retrieved December 2007 (http://www.sliceofscifi.com/2007/05/24/manga-nobel-prize.)

Solomon, Charles. "Four Mothers of Manga Gain American Fans with Expertise in a Variety of Visual Styles." *New York Times*, November 28, 2006. Retrieved November 2007 (http://www.nytimes.com/2006/11/28/arts/design/28clam.html?_r=1&ref=television&oref=slogin).

Thompson, Jason. *Manga: The Complete Guide*. New York, NY: Del Rey, 2007.

Web Japan. "Exploring the History of Manga: Kyoto Museum Shares Comic Culture with the World." Trends in Japan, January 22, 2007. Retrieved November 2007 (http://web-japan.org/trends/arts/art070122.html).

Index

About the Author

Tamra Orr is the author of more than one hundred nonfiction books for children of all ages. She is a full-time author, and when she gets the chance, she reads everything she can get her hands on. Orr lives in the Pacific Northwest with her husband and her four children, most of whom are all avid manga fans.

Photo Credits

Cover, p. 41 Kazuhiro Nogi/AFP/Getty Images; pp. 4, 6, 18, 29, 39, 56, 57, 59, 60, 62 (top left) © www.istockphoto.com/Janne Ahvo; p. 7 © age fotostock/SuperStock; pp.12, 44 SIPA/Newscom; pp. 17, 54 Jens Schlueter/AFP/Getty Images; p. 19 Réunion des Musées Nationaux/Art Resource, NY; p. 20 The Four Immigrants Manga by Henry Yoshitaka Kiyama. Courtesy of Stone Bridge Press; p. 22 William West/AFP/Getty Images; p. 24 Kyodo News/Newscom; p. 27 John MacDougall/AFP/Getty Images; p. 30 El Universal/Especial/Newscom; p. 33 © Frank Carter/Lonely Planet Images; p. 34 © AP Images; p. 46 © Annebicque Bernard/Corbis Sygma; p. 49 © Volkmar Schulz/Keystone Press/Zuma Press; p. 50 Junko Kimura/Getty Images

Photo Researcher: Cindy Reiman